Enhancing Early Years Science

Enhancing Early Years Science

Jennifer Smyth

Trentham Books

Stoke on Trent, UK and Sterling, USA

Trentham Books Limited
Westview House   22883 Quicksilver Drive
734 London Road   Sterling
Oakhill   VA 20166-2012
Stoke on Trent   USA
Staffordshire
England ST4 5NP

First published 2007

British Library Cataloguing-in-Publication Data
A catalogue record for this book is available from the British Library

ISBN: 978 1 85856 387 9

Cover picture: Sado Lauren and other photographs by Steve Smyth

Designed and typeset by Trentham Print Design Ltd, Chester and
printed in Great Britain by Cromwell Press Ltd, Trowbridge.

Contents

This book is dedicated to my father who was
my inspiration to teach

Acknowledgements

I would like to thank Jo and Tom for providing me with such a rich source of Early Years experience and for their continued love and support. I must also mention my niece, Ruth who worked hard on the final indexing and tidying up of the script. Also to my friends within the Primary department of London Metropolitan University who provided advice and encouragement. To the staff and children from my time at St.John's Primary, especially Tim and Lydia who worked tirelessly to achieve our Science Garden Dream and to Charlotte who provided valuable help with issues of Literacy. To Louise and her class from Sacred Heart Primary School. Also to Sado Lauren for providing a wonderful cover picture. My grateful thanks to Gillian for her help and gentle coaxing and finally to Steve for his patience and good humour and without whom I would never have started on such an adventure.

Foreword

This is an inspiring book. The text covers essential areas that will enhance the teaching of science in the Early Years. The author has applied her skills, knowledge and experience in 'getting into the minds' of young children. She has developed and promoted models of good practice and innovative ways of delivering the curriculum. In addition the book has been presented in such a way that it integrates science into the other essential areas of teaching, namely: literacy, numeracy and technology. Through these approaches, Jen has been able to write a book that is both informative and reflective and can help provide a firm base for early years practitioners. The book should help enthuse and develop young 'enquiring minds'. Enthusiasm for science that is properly nurtured at this stage is a way to provide and motivate our budding scientists who will contribute to our future, and to the science and technology economy.

Prof. Chris Branford White
Director of IHRP
London Metropolitan University

Section 1
Introduction

The ideal education for a young man has a strong emphasis on encouraging free expression and natural playfulness. Is it nothing to jump, play, run all day? He will never be so busy in his life. (Rousseau 1762)

1
Why this book?

What do I hope to achieve in this book?

In my role as a primary science lecturer at London Metropolitan University I am frequently asked about suitable resources, including books, to help teachers or students in the classroom. There are many but I felt that what was needed was one which looks holistically at the whole concept of young children acquiring scientific concepts and skills . How do they learn? How can we make this acquisition of vital skills, an active, exciting process for children and adults alike? As the title suggests I am offering suggestions for extending and enhancing existing practice.

Science is boring, complicated, elitist – these words are associated with science in general. Unfortunately these criticisms are well earned moan – communication isn't always a priority in the world of science, and scientists are stereotypically portrayed as white, middle class, male and introvert. I happen to be married to such an apparently stereotypical creature and he and I have both worked tirelessly over many years to overcome the negative issues surrounding science and present it as an exciting, enjoyable and relevant area of learning.

I hope in this book to share my enthusiasm and passion for fostering love of for this subject in children as early as possible in their school lives. This book is not intended to be a definitive programme of work. It is a means of extending and enhancing the excellent practice that goes on in many early years settings.

The nature of science in the early years is such that it is inextricably linked to Design and Technology and although I have devoted a chapter to Science and D&T, the two areas of the curriculum are continually interwoven and it would

3

be difficult to imagine carrying out many science investigations without also mentioning aspects of D&T.

What is the vision?

This book is a call to arms for early years practitioners. Not an exhortation to start teaching 'science' or to suddenly add more 'engineering' to your practice. Instead, a challenge to recognise that the so called STEM subjects (Science, Technology, Engineering and Maths) are already there in early years teaching – and that some of the best science (and other STEM) teaching happens in classrooms with 3 to 7 year-olds.

As I complete this book late in 2006, yet another cry goes up from industry that schools are failing to produce the scientists that the UK needs. The implication is that schools are leaving science to wither away while the children have fun expressing themselves through painting and poetry. Yet in any nursery classroom you will see young engineers in action, as plastic bricks are nonchalantly converted into houses, and furniture rearranged to model the interior of a jumbo jet. Listen to the buzz of conversation and you soon realise that hypotheses are being put forward and experiments performed – perhaps catalysed by that familiar prompt 'Shall we find out?'

The problem is that much of this brilliant teaching goes unrecognised. A lot of it isn't even recognised as such by the practitioners who have brought it about – to them it is just sound, sensible practice. Building bricks have always been part of the early years classroom. Curiosity has always been a much prized attribute of young children.

What we need to do is two-fold. We need to build on young children's propensity to explore and manipulate their environment, so that they are confident in their approach to science in later years of education. And we need to influence practice through the rest of the primary school and through secondary education too so that the early years approach to science becomes part of standard practice and is not patronisingly dismissed as 'just play'.

And all children should be made to feel that science is for them and about them. The stereotype of the white male scientist has implications for children's learning. If the curriculum seems always to be about other people but never about them, they may well switch off. But as Robin Richardson {2004} observes: 'science is a universal human achievement, not something which is distinctively western'. He urges that scientific skills and concepts be illustrated with regard to 'issues of global interdependence, shared humanity, difference, diversity, conflict and justice'. In *Here, There and Everywhere*, Richardson devotes pages 48 to 55 to illustrating how science and technology can be presented in the inclusive way for which he argues.

The CGFS document, built upon the recommendations in *Early Learning Goals* (1999) is equally clear:

> This guidance is intended to help practitioners plan to meet the diverse needs of all children... No child should be excluded or disadvantaged because of ethnicity, culture, religion, home language, family background, special educational needs, disability, gender or ability.

An inclusive approach is entirely fitting in a subject that is about inquiry, finding out for oneself, challenging assumptions. And, as Esme Glauert (1994) argues, this approach is 'equally vital in monolingual, monocultural schools' – although the case studies which follow here all took place in culturally diverse schools. All I need to add is that science and technology have equal relevance to girls and boys. An inclusive approach to both the subject and the learners characterises this book.

The first assignment I set my students of primary teaching at London metropolitan is to make a Big Book to use in the classroom that challenges the stereotype of the scientist.

Why me?

Now that's a good question. I've been interested in approaches to science education ever since I trained as a teacher. In the early 1990s I was fortunate to work with the British Association for the Advancement of Science as they extended their Young Investigators science clubs to include material for Key Stage 1. These early ideas grew into the First Investigators clubs (see Appendix), which have been so successful, and are now being incorporated in Primary CREST (CREative Science and Technology).

The first National Science Week was held in 1994, at about the time I was working with the BA. Science Minister William Waldegrave was looking for somewhere to launch the concept. A school was needed, preferably one within three or four miles of Westminster. Would mine be interested? Well you don't miss out on a chance like that, even though the logistics and security turned the place upside down for a week. And the experience taught me how important simple, colourful science activities can be in conveying complex ideas to the community.

A few years later I was awarded a millennium fellowship to work on a community science club for the Brixton area. This brought me into contact with even more specialists in the world of science education, and convinced me that what we call Early Years Science is crucial to understanding our technological world – not just for the children but for everybody.

Since 1998, I have had the privilege of working with trainee teachers, listening to their enthusiasms and advising them on how to shape their energy as they go out to early years classrooms. The position has also enabled me to visit many excellent schools in London, and to see teaching that takes my breath away in its brilliance and imagination.

I have tried to pull together this varied experience into this book. I did not want to write, yet another book on 'How to Teach Science', because there are so many. Some are very good indeed, but I wanted to approach science from a different standpoint, to produce a book that celebrated existing practice and took it to the next level. A book that would be useful for students and practitioners alike, and might also find a space on the shelves of education officers at museums or science centres.

Why a book like this?

Even though this is not a standard textbook, it is worth re-iterating the theory that underpins science education. So chapters 2 and 3 are quick visits to the subject of what science is and what science education is about. Experienced practitioners may want to skip over these and refer to them later.

Next comes a section called Approaches. These are my main enthusiasms, the major lessons I have learned. Finally, in the section labelled Knowledge and Understanding I cover the relationship between science and other subjects on the curriculum, the vitally important area of equal opportunities and conclude with a final chapter on resources and materials.

2

How do young children learn?

How do we start to learn Science?

From the very earliest days in its life a child develops beliefs about the things that happen in its surroundings. The baby lets go of the rattle and it falls to the ground; it does it again and the pattern repeats itself. It pushes a ball and it goes on rolling across the floor. In this way, sets of expectations are established which enable the child to begin to make predictions. Initially these are isolated and independent of one another. However as the child grows older, all its experiences of pushing, pulling, lifting, throwing and feeling and seeing things stimulate the development of more generalised sets of expectations and the ability to make predictions about a wider range of experiences. By the time the child receives formal teaching in science it has already constructed a set of beliefs about a wide range of natural phenomena. (Driver *et al*, 1985)

As Ros Driver and her colleagues observe, children are interested in their surroundings from a very early age and continually react with them, acquiring new investigative skills which they refine as they mature. For example, young children can discriminate between things that move on their own and those that need pushing. They also begin to realise that if objects are dropped they will fall downwards. With every action a child is able to make they are constructing theories which are continually being refined when they engage in new related inquiries.

The following observation illustrates the refining of ideas which is part of the learning process. The children are in Reception class and have been carrying out an investigation with cars and slopes. They experimented with different strengths of pushes (1 finger, 2 fingers etc) and asked to predict how far the car would roll. After the initial investigation, the teacher introduced different textures on the slope and the children were again asked to predict the distances the car would travel. Although the concept of friction is not usually introduced at this stage the children were able to start thinking about why the cars performed differently according to the surface they were on. The practical session was reinforced with an appropriate computer game. The class had been working on The Circus and the teacher challenged the children to create a trampoline for marbles to jump off into a beaker.

Case Study 1
Marbles

Jasmine and Yusef have put together a Correx slope, a 'trampoline' (which they call a bouncer) and a catching cup.

Yusef: Try now.

Jasmine: Missed. It missed the bouncer.

Yusef: The bouncer has to be nearer. (*moves it*) Try again.

Jasmine: That one missed as well.

Yusef: You didn't start that one from the top. It wasn't going as fast.

Jasmine: Here's another one.

Yusef: That was close.

Jasmine: It hit the bouncer, but it missed the cup. Move the cup.

Yusef: (*moves cup*) Go! (*marble bounces over cup*)

Jasmine: Move the cup back.

Yusef: (*moves cup again*) Go... (*misses again*)

Jasmine: Too much.

Yusef moves cup again.

Jasmine: This one...

Yusef: Yes! Do it again... (*second marble goes in cup*). Yes

Jasmine: Miss, we've done it. Come and see.

Teacher: Does it work?

Yusef: Every time...

As Glauert, Heal and Cook in their paper 'Knowledge and understanding of the world' observe:

> From their earliest years young children observe and interact with their im-
> mediate physical environment. They follow the movement of toys as adults
> play with them or reach out and feel objects. As their motor skills increase
> they push and pull things, make sounds by banging or shaking.

Early years practitioners are aware of the commonly held misconception that teaching in Early Years classrooms is minimal and that Early Years practitioners are no more than child minders who work in a school or nursery setting. It is an easily acquired misconception. Any lively early years setting will give an immediate impression that the children are engaging in various forms of apparently unstructured play and that the staff are merely interested bystanders. But something quite different is going on.

This misinterpretation of the role of early years educators continues: older children are perceived as needing the 'best teachers' and the younger children can make do with less able teachers. I have seen this in operation. After teaching the Nursery and the Reception class for some years I decided to move into Year 6. This was generally accepted as the year which the Deputy Head taught and as I had just been appointed to this position I was expected to move upwards. The Year 6 children were initially quite mistrustful of my ability to teach them. I heard several of them mutter during the first few days about not having a proper teacher, but eventually I was accepted.

The whole concept of play continues to be contentious in the education world. Some outside the early years see play as a time-filler, an activity that requires teachers to do little preparation. The pressure placed on schools by the National Curriculum in the late 1980s to perform to given levels had an adverse effect on early years teaching, especially Years 1 and 2. Many schools abandoned home corners, water play/sand play and insisted that the children should be taught in more rigid ways. The introduction of the CGFS in May 2000 brought the Foundation stage into line with the rest of the primary sector, providing a linear pathway from Nursery through to the end of Year 6. This document clearly acknowledges the importance of play in the Foundation stage, where it is a crucial part of learning. As Wood (2004) remarks

> The Foundation Stage has been broadly welcomed by the early childhood
> community because of the emphasis placed on the role and value of play in
> supporting learning at home and in educational settings. Good quality play
> is linked to positive learning outcomes in the cognitive, emotional, social
> and psycho-motor domains.

I was horrified by a literacy lesson I sat in on soon after the Literacy Hour began. The teacher carefully placed a stop clock on the table before starting the session. Most of the children were actively involved in producing a poster to advertise the merits of their school when the clock suddenly buzzed and the teacher immediately stopped the lesson and moved on to something else. The children had already become accustomed to the disjointed manner of teaching and moved on without question. The creative aspect of the work was lost and although the class would return to the poster making in the next day's Literacy Hour, the initial spontaneity would inevitably be lost.

At Key Stage 1 children were expected to perform to tests. The results were announced and the children who hadn't managed to produce the desired results were made to feel inadequate and to feel that their parents too had somehow failed. Parents, meeting informally at the school gates would discuss the performance of the teachers in the style of Match of the Day, swapping children's performances and reinforcing their feelings of inadequacy. But it has at last accepted that describing the activities that take place in the early years setting should be approached separately.

In their paper on revisiting play, Youngquist and Pataray-Ching (2004) contend that the profession needs to establish a different discourse for play that occurs in the early childhood classroom to be interpreted especially by non educators as educational, meaningful, theoretically driven, and curricularly worthwhile in the academic setting. We turn to literature on play and inquiry theory to provide a theoretical lens for our discussion. And to define play that is associated with academic learning, we describe each instance as an act of 'inquiry'. Inquiry, we believe, is a term that connotes critical and reflective thought and promotes the attainment of the intellectual capacity of every learner.

They go on to discuss the need to develop the language for such 'inquiry' so that parents and the general public can better understand how young children acquire an understanding of the world.

In Hutt's model (see Littledyke and Huxford, 1982) play is categorised in three different styles

- *Epistemic play* involving exploration, problem-solving, acquisition of skills and knowledge
- *Ludic play* – involving fantasy, role-play, creative thinking, innovation
- *Games play* – which is rule-based play

Epistemic play is generally seen as the first step towards understanding a situation – the child will ask what something is in order to gain knowledge.

The second or Ludic stage involves the child asking what they can do with the object or experience. The third phase entails the child actively taking part in the experience.

Throughout the stages children actively construct their own understanding of the world, each Inquiry or Play situation adding to this understanding. By building on these experiences children can acquire new skills and knowledge.

Donaldson (1978) presents an excellent summary of this process:

> It is possible to build up a picture of the young human being in which the following are among the most prominent features.
>
> 1. First, he actively tries to make sense of the world from a very early point in his life: he asks questions, he wants to know. (This is evidently so as soon as verbal questions can be formulated. It is probably true even before the language appears.)
>
> 2. Also from a very early stage, the child has purposes and intentions: he wants to do. These questionings and these strivings imply some primitive sense of possibility which reaches beyond a realisation of how they might be.
>
> 3. The sense of the possible which arises in conjunction with wanting to know involves first, a simple realisation of ignorance (there might be a tiger around the corner, I haven't looked) and then an attempt to use considerations of compatibility and incompatibility to extend the field of the known and reduce uncertainty.

Empiricism, Nativism or Interactionism

Much research has been devoted to examining how young children learn, and it is generally agreed that there are three main models which describe children's acquisition of skills and knowledge: empiricist, nativist, interactivist.

Empiricism

This model sees children as empty vessels waiting to be filled – teaching them everything it is assumed they need to know, step by step. This theory assumes that they are not active participants in this process and play only a passive role in their learning. Breaking down actions into smaller pieces may be necessary, but the vital difference between the empiricist standpoint and the other two models is the absence of children's participation.

Nativism

This model suggests that humans are pre-programmed to develop in certain ways. This model accepts that certain areas of children's lives should be held sacrosanct. Bruce (2004) argues that

> Adults can offer help, but in this approach they should never insist upon it. They need to be highly skilled in the way they approach children. The home area in an early years setting is often one such sacrosanct area with walls around it so children can be away from adults in a 'world of their own'. Inevitably this leads to a major emphasis on relationships with adults and peers, based on respect for the child's unfolding development.

Interactionism

This is the most sophisticated of the models describing children: not only do the child's structures interact with each other, but they also alter each other. External interactions occur, as well as internal interaction through the senses.

Interactionism is a two way process between child and adult, the child sometimes taking the lead and at others the adult instigating the conversation or activity. The model of Interactionism allies itself most closely to the type of teaching and learning taking place in our early years settings. It adopts a mixture of Empiricism and Nativism and is strongly influenced by the work of Piaget, Vygotsky and Dunn. Notice too how closely interactionism reflects the model of science learning put forward in the next chapter.

3

What is science and how can
it be enhanced?

Everyone knows what science is, don't they? It's got test tubes and Bunsen burners and microscopes, and smells and bangs and mutant life-forms that threaten the future of world. And we have to know about it so we can buy the right kind of television and know to switch off our mobile phones in garages and buy food that doesn't contain genetically modified crops.

And we know what a scientist looks like. He's a man, white, about forty, bald on top but with a bushy beard beneath, thick black rimmed glasses, wearing a slightly stained white coat with a leaky biro and a metal thingy poking out of the top pocket.

The trouble is, these media short-hands and stereotypes are very pervasive. Children as young as three are exposed to them (watch the portrayals of scientists in children's cartoons) and their parents certainly are. The mother of a five year old may feel complimented by the comment: 'She's a natural athlete.' The parallel comment: 'He's a natural scientist' may be received more equivocally.

There's a good deal of confusion about what science is and why it should be taught. So let's start with a bold statement, one that justifies the prominence we give to science in schools.

Science is the basis of all rational thought. It is the way we know about things.

Now that does make it important. And of course it is worth teaching. Knowing and understanding about things is what school is all about, and it is especially what early years education is about.

And it follows from that definition that science is something we are all involved in. We are all scientists, because we are all rational beings that make decisions based on experience. The fact that some people spend much of their time exploring things which are difficult to understand doesn't make them different. It makes them *professional* scientists, because they are paid to carry out their research. The rest of us are still scientists, because day by day we are adding to our knowledge through that most important source of evidence – experience. And children in their early years are going through this process faster than any other group.

Science as a process

Given the importance of science in our lives, what is surprising is that the process of science is so poorly defined. We know what the end product is, but how do we get there? What exactly enables us to be rational, to be able to know that when we sit on a chair it will support our weight or that when a jet screams down a runway it will carry us into the air?

Let's start a quick tour of the philosophy of science by looking at some basic ideas of how it works. Here's a set of ideas that paraphrase the general public's view of science:

- Scientists do activities and collect lots of data
- They look at the data and work out explanations from them
- Predictions of things that will happen are deduced from theories

We can re-write these as more general statements

- Science as knowledge is derived from the facts of experience
- Science generalises from singular to universal
- Predictions and explanations are deduced from theories

This is a summary of a philosophy called inductivism. It all looks very plausible as set in statements, and we can run a mental test on it by thinking about learning at a simple level:

- I sat on the wooden chair and it did not collapse
- I sat on the armchair and it did not collapse
- All chairs can be sat on
- That chair in the classroom will be safe for me to sit on

There are two problems with inductivism. First – and it's probably the one you have already hit on – is the safety of generalising from the singular to the universal. An older child or an adult might well wish to modify their learning about chairs as follows:

- I remember that chair at grandad's was a bit wobbly
- And that camping chair my mum sat on fell apart
- That chair in the classroom will probably be safe for me to sit on

The second problem is that inductivism tells us nothing about the move from generalisation to theory. It is fine at the level of chairs, but not very useful when it comes to a plane on a runway.

To examine the idea of science a little more, we need to consider what most professional scientists are doing or think they are doing:

- They invent creative explanations for observations
- They test these explanations, trying to show that they are wrong
- An explanation can be described as scientific so long as you can't falsify it, ie prove that it is wrong
- Once falsified, a theory must be discarded
- No theory can be said to be true, only the best explanation available at the time

Once again, we can re-write this as a set of statements:

- Observation is guided by theory
- Theories are speculative conjectures which must be ruthlessly tested
- A theory may exist for as long as it is not falsified
- Once falsified, a theory must be discarded
- No theory can be said to be true, only the best explanation available at the time.

This is a summary of a philosophy known as falsificationism. It was proposed by philosopher Karl Popper. We can turn it into everyday experience as follows:

- Planes fly because they have wings
- Let's build lots and make certain they all fly
- Plane crash. Newspaper headline 'Was the wing at fault?'
- You're not getting me up in that thing...
- It's okay, we've found out it was metal fatigue. We'll build our new planes more strongly and monitor them for faults.

This gets a bit nearer to what science is about, but philosophers would insist that there is yet another step.

- People come up with explanations for observations
- If some of these explanations are wrong, they are described as anomalies and parked for future investigation.
- When there are many anomalies someone will come up with a better explanation
- The new theory will replace the old one
- No theory can be said to be true, only the best explanation available at the time.

This is really a pragmatic modification of falsification, put forward by philosopher Thomas Kuhn. His ideas can be summarised as follows:

- The falsification idea is generally right, but people are unwilling to discard theories that have been useful in the past
- Puzzles that defy solution are regarded as anomalies rather than falsifiers
- When anomalies build up they become a 'crisis'
- Theories only fall after a crisis. This becomes a 'revolution' in thinking.

And in everyday terms this becomes:

- For philosophy students, morning is not observed to exist
- Sometimes there are philosophy lectures in the morning
- This is strange, but it makes no difference to a philosophy degree
- With my philosophy degree I have a good job in the City.
- For which I have to get up at 7 o'clock!

Okay, that's amusing but why is it important?

As teachers, we need to know why we are teaching something. We're not teaching our children vast amounts of facts about things, nor are we training them all to become doctors or research scientists. What we do want are children who will ask intelligent questions about things, and who will develop their powers of rational thought,

Now we know about the underlying philosophies of science, let's take a look at how it can inform our teaching of one of my favourite activities – Blowing Bubbles. Get some liquid detergent, add a little glycerine, find some wands and have fun.

Now let's examine it from an Inductivist perspective.

- Children blow bubbles
- Children make careful observations
- Children record their observations
- Children deduce particulate theory of matter

There may be a modicum of exaggeration about the final statement, but I often feel that this is what politicians and the general public expect of science education. Even experienced teachers on inset courses cannot make the leap from proposition 3 to proposition 4. And it is not because their knowledge is insufficient – it is because the expectation is impossible given what we know about the structure of science.

From the falsificationist perspective we get:

- Children blow bubbles
- Children discuss what they have seen with their peers and their teacher
- Children put forward their own ideas
- Children blow some more bubbles to test their ideas
- Ideas are refined and everyone has fun

Which is a bit closer to the reality of the classroom, but still a little esoteric. Fun is only part of the picture – we want children to have fun, but we also want them to learn. So the final perspective I offer is based on Kuhn's ideas about scientific theories. It is probably the one headteachers and inspectors want to see planned and incorporated into lessons.

- Children blow bubbles
- Children discuss what they have seen with their peers and their teacher
- Children put forward their own ideas
- Children blow some more bubbles to test their ideas
- Teachers introduce theory. More activity.
- Ideas are refined and everyone has fun and learns some science

Just how much theory teachers introduce is up to them and the age and ability of the children for whom the activity is intended. Blowing bubbles is a good activity for all ages; the art of the teacher is in relating the following ideas and questions to particular age groups.

- Bubbles are always round
- Bubbles are full of air
- Bubbles are empty (full of nothing)
- Bubbles have different colours
- The different colours depend on what liquid was used to make them
- Bubbles are thin layers (film) of soap
- The thin film of soap is joined to make a continuous 3-D circle (sphere)
- The soap film traps air inside the sphere
- The soap film and air are very light
- Bubbles will always rise
- The soap film is very thin and this causes the special patterns we see in the surface of bubbles
- When the soap film is pierced the bubble will collapse
- You will get different types of soap film from different mixtures. Some mixtures will give bigger bubbles than others
- Some mixtures will give you more bubbles
- If you trap warm air inside the bubble it will float better than if you trap cold air

Enhancing science

So how can we use these ideas to enhance the experience of science our children receive?

Firstly, we need to give them time, and space to explore. The idea of what this exploration or play should be is investigated in chapter 3. But we also need to give them plenty of equipment and materials to explore – if we are encouraging open ended investigations, we need to recognise that children may ask for virtually anything. Obviously, we cannot supply them with everything – as parents know, children will ask for the moon, but there are strategies for getting them to accept something less. We need to be prepared to anticipate their requests – and to have fall back positions when we cannot provide the elephant or railway locomotive they deem to be so vital. And an even better strategy is to direct curiosity into areas where we can cope with open-ended demands.

We also need to provide plenty of opportunities for talk. Talking to peers, talking to older children, talking to adults; to provide stimulus for ideas and to provide an audience on which to assemble thought processes. Notice that the difference between the inductivist model, which as teachers we instinctively reject, and the falsificationist model is in the refining of ideas – and it is talk that allows young children the capacity to refine ideas.

Also notice the difference between the falsificationist model and the final perspective, to which most early years teachers will instinctively aspire. In the final model, teachers introduce theory. This does not have to be a 'stand at the front' disquisition on particles – it can simply be asking a few questions that will point children in a different direction for their thinking. And the teacher can be any person who is teaching the learner – not necessarily that one professional pulling all the strings in the early years classroom, but a nursery officer, teaching assistant, parent, guest, older child from another class, or simply a peer who may have gained some expertise from an earlier science enhancement.

So what does a science enhancement look like?

It could be anything – but you'll know it when you see it! It could be a visit to a museum, or a factory, or a visit from someone connected with science. But most likely it will involve children in actually doing something. People of all ages learn science best when they can interact with objects – when they can manipulate the objects involved so that they can properly explore the outcomes. So even if you are on a visit to a museum, or someone is coming in to work with the children, interactivity should be at the heart of the experience.

Let me give an example rather than a definition. *Splash!* is a large scale science enhancement, designed to work across the early years age-range. In fact it is fairly easily modified to work across the entire primary range. It consists of a series of activities designed around the theme of water and I used it, with university colleagues, as a way of promoting collaborative work between trainee teachers and the National Maritime Museum.

Over the years, a number of different activities were tried, but eventually four were fixed on because they took roughly the same time – about a quarter of an hour each. This is an important practical point – if you have groups of children engaged in activities, you want each activity to last for the same length of time, otherwise you end up with some children squabbling over equipment and others going completely off-target. All four of the activities are easily set up, interesting, and promote myriad opportunities for discussion between peers and between children and adults. Some of the conversations have been recorded by my students and have been used elsewhere in this book. Each activity could be used separately, as part of other science activities at school or in the wider world.

Best raft

Possibly the easiest activity to set up, and one of the best known. You need a large water container – a storage box is ideal. You can use a bucket, but then you'll only be able to test one boat at a time. Make a boat out of paper, then add marbles one at a time, until the boat sinks. You don't have to use marbles, but they are cheap and convenient. Standard marbles weigh about 8 grams each – if you know of a similar object that is as conveniently heavy and cheap, please let me know!

Children in the early years don't need to do the arithmetic to arrive at an overall weight – they simply need to count the marbles they put in and compare the numbers. Careful folding of an A4 sheet of paper can give a shape that will bear over a hundred marbles – this represents nearly a kilogram in weight. This amazes children and adults alike – if you ask adults beforehand, most will guess that the boat will sink with a load of 10 to 20 marbles. The idea that a one kilogram bag of sugar could be floated is really counter intuitive.

You can try different shapes, and different papers. Old catalogues give good results, because they use glossy papers (on the theory that catalogues will be much thumbed). You can even make your boats out of plastecene – again, it is counter intuitive that a 'heavy' material such as plastecene can be fashioned into a shape that will float.

Best shape

You can also test the best shape for moving through water by towing boat shapes along a length of canal. You can cut the shapes out of correx, or get a parent to make some wooden ones, or buy different shapes in toy shops. You can also buy canal systems from toy shops, or use lengths of guttering, or buy specially made pieces of guttering (from TTS, see appendix). If you are going to use guttering from a DIY store, choose flat-bottomed section – it is more expensive, but it doesn't tip when you put it on the floor. Buying canal systems from toy stores is expensive for this activity, as most systems are sold as sets, and sets contain far more curve sections than straight sections.

Children could time the movement of boats along one section of canal, but the timing and recording are quite difficult for very young children. Instead, it is much more fun to have two lengths of canal side by side and for the children to organise boat races.

You will need to attach strings to the boats, put a weight on the other end of the string and then arrange for the string to pass over a support high enough to give a drop equivalent to the length of the canal. Five-a-side goal posts will do the job.

The great skill children learn from this activity is fair testing – actually getting equal weights on the string, getting the weights to drop at the same time and to drop through the same distance gives much scope for discussion. And there are plenty of things for an adult to prompt discussion about: starting and finishing points, amount of water in canals, how wet the string is.

Best sail

You can also use canals for the children to investigate boats with sails. You will need to modify some boats first of all – you can glue a cotton reel into a toy boat so you can fit a mast into the centre of the cotton reel (the technical term for this is 'stepping the mast'). Using 3mm dowel for the mast means you can easily fit shapes cut from 3mm correx, or you can try and fit more elaborate cloth sails.

Children can easily make a wind generator using a motor with a large propeller already pushed on the shaft and a double AA battery holder, fitted with two AA batteries. When the children touch the motor to the terminals on the battery holder, the propeller spins satisfyingly quickly, producing a good blast of air. Children can use this generated wind to blow the boats along the canal and see which shape sail responds best.

Again, the purpose of the activity is not to get into a deep mathematical investigation of sails. There are many physical factors affecting sail performance, and to investigate them properly you need wind tunnels and test tanks. But the activity does introduce children to simple circuits (you don't need wires to make the fan work), reversible currents (turn the battery holder round and the propeller spins in the other direction) and reversible forces (when the fan turns in the opposite direction the wind moves in the opposite direction – and then the boat moves in the opposite direction). All of which adds up to opportunities for children to recount and possibly record what they have observed.

Best paddle

To complete this suite of activities, we developed an activity where children could make boats very cheaply by fixing two soft-drink bottles together with elastic bands and powering them by putting an elastic band around the neck of the bottle, then winding this band up with a wooden or plastic paddle. The difficulty with this is that if one uses a band round the neck of the bottle, it is difficult to find a paddle small enough not to hit the main body of the bottle as it unwinds. One of my students solved this by fitting 35mm film containers over both bottle necks – this gave enough rigidity to hold an elastic band, and sufficient length to use lolly-sticks as paddles.

These boats work remarkably well for such simple equipment – you just need a big enough area to let them show how well they move. A paddling pool is ideal, especially one with a rigid frame. It is possible to construct a Coke bottle boat that will travel the length of a 2-metre paddling pool on forty winds of an elastic band. Again, the importance of the activity is not so much in the transfer of energy from one form to another, but in the discussion of fair testing that arises when children compare the performance of different boats.

I have approached chapters 2 and 3 from totally different perspectives. Chapter 2 runs through the arguments about play from an early years education perspective. Chapter 3 describes science learning from the viewpoint of the philosophy of science. Yet, encouragingly both arrive at a similar model of learning through doing and talk. And that is the basis of best practice in early years education.

Section 2
Approaches

4

Paired and Peer Teaching

The scene is a familiar one. A hot afternoon, a smallish classroom and thirty tired Year 1 children. Teacher and children alike have tried hard to remain on task but irritability and exhaustion are affecting everyone. Help is at hand, the teacher has forgotten that this afternoon a year 5 child is coming to read the class a story. The older pupil, Amanda arrives and immediately several sleepy children become more animated. The teacher brings the remains of the set lesson to a close and then asks the children to gather on the carpet. Amanda has chosen a book and is ready to read to the class. Silence descends and the children listen attentively to her, behaviour control is perfect, voices aren't raised and the eagerness of the class to listen to everything Amanda has to say is evident throughout the reading. At the close of the story the children are anxious to answer the questions Amanda asks about the story. Several children request a rerun of the book, a request readily agreed and so once more the seemingly exhausted year 1 children are sitting expectantly and quietly waiting for Amanda to begin again.

This isn't a unique scenario. Quite a few schools create opportunities for older children to work alongside younger children on certain activities. In the school I worked in for many years we decided to take the idea of paired teaching one step further by creating a scheme to pair up Key Stage 2 classes with foundation and early years classes for the purpose of reading together. The scheme had to be set up with great care as the initiative could only succeed if all the children taking part benefited. Careful pairing of Key Stage 2 with early years children was needed to ensure that experiences would be positive. Pairing decisions needed to take account of the abilities of the two children involved – whether or not the older child was confident and would be able to cope with the younger one's reading needs. If not, the pairing might need

adjusting. The scheme sought to avoid damaging the self esteem of the older child so both children's needs had to be carefully assessed.

This chapter considers the history of peer teaching, then describes case studies of schools in which I've used it to convey scientific concepts.

Historical perspectives

At the end of 18th century, philanthropist Joseph Lancaster created a school for poor children after he found teaching in a boarding school to be very un-satisfactory. The school was started in his father's home in Southwark in 1798 but it soon proved so popular that in 1801 he had to find bigger premises in Borough Road.

So many boys wished to attend his school that he found it impossible to manage the teaching efficiently. And the cost of maintaining such an enterprise ensured that Lancaster was continually seeking funding and was forced to develop another method of delivering the teaching. He resorted to an early form of peer teaching. More able boys were used to teach the younger and less able. He travelled all over England establishing similar schools, with financial support from benefactors such as Josiah Wedgewood and Henry Brougham and many of the non-conformist philanthropists of the day. However Lancaster found himself in continual need of funding, as the need for schooling for the poor was far greater than he was able to provide. Eventually the school movement he had initiated was rescued from financial disaster by several of Lancaster's loyal supporters. The Royal Lancastrian Society was replaced by the British and Foreign School Society. The central idea of using more able pupils to teach less able children continued to be used for teaching large numbers of children when there were very few teachers.

Today many countries use peer tutoring. It is popular in the United States but the American scheme carries with it many issues that don't fit easily with the central ideal: the tutoring is strictly monitored, the work highly prescriptive and it appears to be more about using pupils in place of, rather than as well as, professional teachers.

Research carried out by Bronfenbrenner (1970) noted:

> In the Soviet Union there is much involvement by adults and older children in the social life of youngsters; Soviet children are explicitly taught in school to help each other, and especially to help younger children. Classes of older children often 'adopt' a younger class, and older children help younger children with school work and by reading stories to them. The adoption system is extended to the world of grown-ups – a factory, shop or office takes responsibility for a class of school children.

The idea that pupils benefit from working with their peer group or paired with an older or younger child furthers our understanding of the development of children's ability (see Chapter 2). The ideas underpinning paired teaching are drawn from theorists who explored children's developmental skill, notably Piaget, Vygotsky and Bruner. The essence of their research and its relevance to teaching today are discussed in chapter 2. From the standpoint of paired teaching it is useful to look at the work on pedagogy carried out by Vygotsky and continued by Bruner. Vygotsky stated that within the model of human learning is the ZPD or Zone of Proximal Development. When children are presented with a task, they can operate on their own at a certain level, but they are able to perform at a higher level when a more able peer or older child or indeed an adult is present. They can perform better if 'scaffolded' by this more able person. Bruner introduced the term 'scaffolding' to describe help of this kind.

The benefits of children working with 'a more able other' are defined in various ways: *The zone of actual development* (Vygotsky, 1978 p86) *defines functions that have already matured, that is, the end product of development.* Vygotsky sees this development as the child working independently without any influence from others.

The zone of potential or proximal development *'defines those functions that have not yet matured but are in the process of maturation, functions that will mature tomorrow but are currently in an embryonic state'* (Bruce, 2004). The child has reached the edge of their own ability to learn something but will be able to increase and develop their understanding with the help of a more able peer or adult.

The zone of future development describes what the child will be able to do on their own at a later point of development. As Whitbread (1996) maintains:

> More recent research inspired by Vygotsky's work has argued that there is a much more central role for the adult, and indeed, for other children, in the processes of learning. This role is not as an instructor delivering knowledge, however, but rather as a 'scaffolder'.

Paired tutoring has the following

- ■ it frees up teacher time – the class teacher is able to concentrate on other children
- ■ it builds the confidence of the tutor
- ■ it creates new friendships, which usually extend beyond the actual teaching time
- ■ it increases opportunities for the less able or younger child to learn
- ■ it develops social skills on both sides
- ■ it is cheap to set up
- ■ it is relatively easy to monitor
- ■ it can target specific areas of need and work exclusively on the targeted areas when required

Peer tutoring improves the attainment in the tutored subject area of both the tutor and the tutee. Although the tutors may once again be covering material they had presumed to have mastered, there are nevertheless gains from this process. The tutors may be reviewing and consolidating existing knowledge, filling in gaps, finding extra meanings and be formulating their knowledge into new conceptual frameworks. Above all, they are likely to remember the material better from experience of the need to put knowledge to some purpose. (Topping, 1998)

But paired tutoring can also have disadvantages

- Tutors will model their teaching styles on those of their own teachers – therefore it is essential that positive modeling is in place

- Tutoring can interfere with a tutor's own learning – careful organisation of timetable is essential to ensure this doesn't happen

- If able children act as tutors to less able children of same age it is usually unsuccessful – the learners perceive themselves as failures.

As educators we are aware of the processes involved in children learning from one another. There is research about it but my interest was in looking at it from the perspective of early acquisition of scientific concepts.

Case study 2

When doing research in the school I was teaching in, I had worked with Year 5 children working alongside Year 1 children on a science investigation. The area of earth and space isn't part of the early years curriculum, but the fact is that all children experience night and day and questions about this are frequently raised. The seeming passage of the sun across the sky and the forming of shadows is seldom understood. Accordingly, I created an activity in which a Year 5 child and a Year 1 child would work together on looking at shadows and the changes in their length during the course of a day. I spent a lesson working with the older pupil on the practical explanation of shadow formation and when she felt sure she knew and understood about it, I asked her to explain the concept to the younger pupil. Since young children work best with materials that are found within their everyday life, we used a school PE hoop, a Lego person and a torch.

> The context within which scientific ideas are presented is vitally important in motivating children and ensuring that the ideas connect with their own lives sufficiently to make sense. (Howe, Davis *et al*, 2003)

Using these everyday objects we were able to demonstrate how the shadows changed in length during the day. Although the concept was fairly complex for a six year old, the older pupil was able to help him grasp the basic concept. She had to learn how to explain the processes involved and to examine her own knowledge and understanding of this area in order to translate this knowledge for the younger child. Thus the outcome of this activity was a learning process for both pupils.

Although space on a busy timetable is always at a premium, this idea of paired learning can be used in a broader context too. Each Friday afternoon, when many schools still try to allow time for personal choice or choosing time, it is possible to set up areas of interest and provide opportunities for investigations. If timetabling allows, it also enables class teachers to develop their own particular expertise and a chance to work with children of all age groups. Other areas had Art, History and D&T as their central theme. I was responsible for science investigations.

The afternoons provided opportunities for children to work together on projects across the entire age range from Nursery to Year 6. This was a forerunner of the Community science clubs established later. During these special times all the children had to play active roles in whichever area they had chosen. Older pupils weren't there just to supervise the younger ones – they needed to extend their own expertise and knowledge as well as helping the younger children to learn. Key Stage 2 pupils were paired with Key stage 1 and Foundation age pupils. The pairs worked together on Friday afternoons, each child in the pair bringing their own expertise to the challenges we set them. The pairs sometimes decided to work with other pairs, but in each session paired learning formed the focus of the afternoons.

Case Study 3
The first science project we worked on aimed to give children an active role in the re-design and construction of the school garden.

Although in the centre of Brixton, our school was fortunate to have a fair sized garden. But it had been the victim of numerous staff changes and interests and was in a contained but uninteresting state. The schoolkeeper was invited to join discussions with the children and interested staff members.

We had applied for a grant to improve the garden and received a reasonable sum of money to begin work. The early years pupils worked in pairs on the design of the new garden. We discussed the requirements for the garden and considered the ways it could be used once it was established. The younger children often had more adventurous ideas than the older children and their imaginative ideas were discussed and incorporated into the design where possible. But some were totally impractical – like creating a miniature farm where goats, rabbits, mice and even a horse would be kept! Looking after the class pet, be it a guinea pig, rabbit or mouse, had always been problematic during holidays and at weekends and the idea of finding volunteers to act as unpaid farmhands was too daunting to be considered.

The gardening teams were asked to come up with ideas for specific areas of the gardens. We already had a large pond but this was little used, and an un-appealing wire mesh cover had been hurriedly fitted after vandals had entered the school premises and one unfortunate intruder had fallen in. The intruder had actually tried to sue the school. So the pond would have to have a cover if the garden was to be more accessible to the children. It was decided that the pond and the surrounding ground could be made into an attractive focus point. Discussions were held by the pairs to decide what was needed in terms of planting and stocking the pond and how it could be used as a resource for making learning more interesting. The groups made sketches and held discussions with the schoolkeeper about the planting around its perimeter. The perimeter was duly planted up with suitable plants and bulbs and the children set up rotas to ensure that new stock was properly looked after.

The pairs then went on to look at ways of using the pond for dipping. Safety considerations were discussed and it was decided that three places would have special platforms for the children to dip their nets. Although building the platforms was a specialist job, the schoolkeeper, a keen gardener and pond specialist, built them quickly himself and to the specifications asked for by the children.

Another area of the grounds was to form the wild area. The children decided to create this space to encourage garden wildlife to colonise. The area would be left out of the planting scheme in order to encourage natural colonisation.

Most areas of the garden were laid out as conventional beds but these weren't easily accessible to young children. Once again discussions were held and eventually it was agreed that some small raised beds could be created – each early years class would be given their own bed and the children involved in the gardening project would be designated an early years class to look after and record their progress.

The project grew bigger each term and the children soon decided to hold a gardening club once a week during lunchtimes. Once again older children worked with younger children in joint learning situations – to excellent effect.

After a while one of the older pupils suggested that we create a trail around the garden for visitors and the children not involved in the scheme to follow.

This provided an excellent incentive for considering the varying needs and ensuring that the trail would be accessible. The pairs devised clues and questions about the trail for the leaflet they produced for use in the garden. The friendships created during this time were symbiotic in nature, each child gaining valuable knowledge and experience from the collaboration. Ample cross-curricular opportunities were provided and these are discussed in other chapters, but the garden certainly responded to the requirements of the *Primary National Strategy – Excellence and Enjoyment in Schools* (2003). The CGFS offers a more holistic approach to the curriculum and assumes that learning in school is naturally cross-curricular, so schemes such as the garden are useful for delivering teaching and learning of this kind.

While the scheme continued, other science projects were introduced. A water recycling project was set up, pairing the younger children with older ones and the partnerships were almost always fruitful. As with all initiatives, some re-assignment of partners was required but usually the original pairing continued and this seems to have strengthened the feeling of cohesion created by pupils working together across the classes.

During the paired science lessons children explored different methods of recording the work they were doing. These collaborative sessions increased the confidence and interest of all concerned, regardless of their individual levels of ability – again confirming Vygotsky's research on children working with a more able other.

An initiative called SEEDS was created by a team of science communication specialists on this idea and on paired teaching and learning, which SEEDS (Sustainable Environmental Education Development Sessions) clubs were devised in which Year 5 pupils would run a science club for Year 2 pupils. Ideally, the older pupils are trained at the end of their 4th year so that they are ready to start the clubs as soon as they enter Year 5 or, as the trainers prefered, at the beginning of Year 5 with the intention of enabling the older pupils to start the clubs right away. It is hoped that using Year 5 pupils will make the scheme self sustaining. At the end of each year the Year 5 pupils will train up the Year 4 pupils to take over in the following year.

A major feature of the project is the large and colourful box which contains most of the items needed for the 30 suggested activities. Most are non-consumables so, after the initial cost, the clubs can be delivered virtually free in subsequent years. After a training day provided by the SEEDS team, the Year 5 pupils are sent back to their schools and encouraged to set up their club, bringing in Year 2 pupils as club members. The clubs are carefully structured.

Equipment is provided and the trainers give training and monitor the club sessions to check on successes and problems that arise. Feedback is sought from both the providers (Year 5) and the consumers (Year 2). Those taking part in the clubs are encouraged to produce new ideas and can join in the British Association First and Young Investigators schemes which encourage children from early years onwards to work towards various awards. (These are currently being rewritten.) The older children can also work towards a Science Communicators award. For an excellent example of paired learning see the Sphere Science web-site at http://www.spherescience.co.uk/)

The case studies described in this chapter could be introduced in school and early years settings. Paired learning offers social and academic advantages to all the pupils involved in the schemes.

5

Creating effective home/ school partnerships

This chapter explores the differing approaches and attitudes adopted towards parents and carers in early years settings. I use the term parent to cover any person who plays a major role in caring for the child outside the school/nursery.

Why such a partnership?

The involvement of parents in the schooling of their children has always been contentious. Raymont (1937) quotes Plato, who, in the 4th century BC, was amongst the first to record his observations about the development of children. Plato believed that 'a child for its own sake was to be taken from its parents and placed under the care of nurses skilled in the art of rearing children'.

Raymont himself (1937) is more moderate. He sees the role of parent and nursery as to work together cooperatively to produce the most successful conditions for a child to develop, observing that:

> The argument that nursery schools tended to sap the sense of parental responsibility was proved to have no foundation in fact. On the contrary that sense of responsibility was quickened and enhanced by being shared with kind and capable 'nurse teachers'.

During the late 19th and early 20th centuries Margaret and Rachel Macmillan worked tirelessly with parents and children, first in the poor areas of Bradford and then in London's inner city. They acknowledged the crucial role of parents in the health and education of children and the necessity of working in partnership with them. They campaigned with Katherine Glaisier to provide free school meals and this resulted in the 1906 Provision of Free School Meals Act. The sisters were instrumental in setting up the first school clinic and later, in 1914, the open air nursery in Peckham.

Sadly, such acknowledgement of the importance of parental involvement was only applicable to parents whose children were underachieving. But it has gradually begun to be seen as a positive aspect of learning once more. Parents should be actively involved in school life whenever possible. Because contact with parents had been made only when problems arose, home/school relationships were not seen as positive or desirable.

Although the Plowden Report of 1967 advocated involving parents in the classroom, little help was given as to how this would be achieved. It offered no guidance on how to stimulate the involvement of parents who were traditionally wary of the role of school – usually because of their own school experience or because of the way schools stereotype certain groups.

With the CGFS (2000), the role of parents in the schooling of their children was once again highlighted:

> Parents (/Carers) are children's first and most enduring educators. When parents and practitioners work together in early years settings, the results have a positive impact on the child's development and learning. Therefore, each setting should seek to develop an effective partnership with parents/carers. effective partnership with parents/carers). (CGFS, 2000)

The importance of a partnership between parent and the school/nursery setting was affirmed further by the Sure Start programmes, established in 2000 in response to the Government Green Paper (1998) which examined the needs of early years children. It is now an accepted view that active involvement of parents in the learning of their children will have a positive impact and that this should start as early as possible. The ten year programme drew on and adapted the Early Headstart programmes already in place in many urban areas of the US, which had proved very successful.

Evaluations are now being carried out to ascertain the success or failure of such schemes. The programmes are set up in areas of socio-economic disadvantage and are meant to literally create a Sure Start for the children living in these areas:

> It aims to ensure delivery of free education for all three and four year olds; affordable, quality childcare and after-school activities in every area; and children's centres and health and family support, particularly in disadvantaged areas where they are most needed (www.surestart.gov.uk)

In the government report *Every Child Matters – change for children* (2003), the place of parents in the education of children was again emphasised as central and crucial to the optimal development of the child.

Parents, carers and families are the most important determinant of children and young people's outcomes. The Change for Children programme aims to ensure that support for parents becomes routine, particularly at key points in a child's life. The initiative addresses the need to embrace all agencies and individuals who may be involved in the child's development, arguing that this should ensure that each child will be given the support they need to develop successfully. The report argues that a child should have the support to

- be healthy
- stay safe
- enjoy and achieve
- make a positive contribution
- achieve economic well being

Whilst acknowledging the need for a more holistic approach towards the welfare of children, it maintains the crucial need for parental involvement:

> Success in the education of children depends, at least in some part, on the involvement of their parents. If a child sees that their parents are enthusiastic about education, they are far more likely to view their schooling in a positive light, and be more receptive to learning. (The Standards Site – Parental involvement)

Why do parents get involved in schools and early years centres?

The reasons for parental involvement are likely to be a combination of

- genuine interest in the education of their child
- single parents especially feeling isolated
- the perception by some parents that because they have passed through the education system they are all experts about education.

The advantages and disadvantages of parental involvement

- Insight is gained into the culture of the classroom, which will appear very different to the classrooms remembered from their own childhood
- Parents who feel isolated can find a sense of belonging
- Teachers come to understand more fully the cultural differences and

similarities among pupils due to the opportunities for school and home to discover more about each other

■ The chances of misconceptions are reduced on either side about the role and life of the school and of misunderstandings arising at school or at home. Matters are more likely to be solved amicably, and children benefit from home and school working in harmony

■ Another pair of hands is available in the classroom to help in the routine of the classroom

■ It may help to settle a child who finds it difficult to be in a classroom – although this doesn't always work.

There are however, some disadvantages of parental involvement in schools:

■ Parents who find it impossible to take an active role in school life because of the pressure of their job or other children can feel they don't belong to the school

■ To parents in some cultures, participation in school life is seen as a part of their child's life which is quite separate from their life in the home

■ Some parents feel uneasy about their child being 'taught' by non-teachers and this sometimes causes anxiety over confidentiality about their child's progress

■ Some teachers feel uneasy about non-professionals apparently doing their job. Gillian Pugh (1996) observes that: 'for example, if practitioners have a view of themselves as the expert on children's learning they may find it difficult to value the parent's views. Often practitioners who feel confident in their work with children feel less confident in their work with parents.'

■ The use of parents in the classroom setting requires an extra level of managerial skill which not all teachers are willing to take on

■ The children whose parents are unwilling or unable to contribute to the classroom may resent the fact that they are not included

Other adults

Adults other than parents can provide a wonderful resource in the classroom. Older people can contribute to the richness of experience and provide a grandparent figure for the children – especially welcome for children who don't live close to their grandparents. Bringing retired people into the classroom through schemes run by Age Concern and CSV have proved beneficial to the pupils and helped to raise the profile of the school in the local community. When children work in a meaningful way with older people the experience can be mutually beneficial.

Case Study 4

As part of an ongoing initiative to raise its profile in the community, my school in Brixton, South London contacted CSV (Community Service Volunteers) and together we set up a project encouraging local retired people to work as volunteers in the school. We launched it with a tea party for the potential participants, organised by Year 6 children. Representatives from the CSV led a short discussion about the role of volunteers in the school.

Several retired people in the neighbourhood became involved with the school. They provided richness of life experience that was warmly received by children and staff alike. The volunteers worked with individual children across the school who had been identified as needing extra input on various parts of their learning.

The project was successful on many levels – the children benefited from one to one contact with an older person and the volunteers were able to work with young children in a meaningful way. The input of the sessions was carefully organised by the teacher and volunteer. Content varied according to need, but proved to be mutually beneficial in all cases.

Extra adult help in school traditionally takes the form of listening to a child read or helping out with maths problems. But we encouraged some of our elderly helpers to become involved in the construction of a new area of the school gardens. They achieved a great deal working with the children, mainly early years classes. Their gardening expertise and patience afforded much needed extra help to our schoolkeeper, who had already been working effectively with groups of children on the environmental project in the school grounds, such as the water recycling initiative which was a central feature of the garden and an excellent resource for the entire school. It was especially rewarding when the garden project won a London school garden prize.

The scheme worked well during the summer months – the volunteers felt confident about moving around a challenging area of Brixton on bright sunny days. But they were less eager to come to the school on bleak autumnal and winter afternoons when it was almost dark.

Although the project only lasted for one summer term, two of the team continued working on individual projects for the rest of the year. It was a good example of how effectively older people can contribute to the life of a school.

Parents and Science

Their own experiences of early schooling leave many parents anxious when their children start school. This is especially true in inner city areas where cultures bring their own clearly defined expectations of the school system. Some of these ideas are embraced by schools but some parents remain reluctant to take an active role in their children's schooling.

So how do we provide an encouraging and welcoming environment where parents feel secure enough to talk about their anxieties over school matters? If these feelings are not discussed it can affect their children's confidence too. There is a particular need to address this problem in the area of the curriculum covering Knowledge and Understanding of the World (CGFS) or Science Key Stage 1. Science conjures up for some parents dreadful images of laboratories, stony faced teachers speaking a language all their own, and their own feelings of inadequacy or disinterest. The relevant research indicates that such anxiety can have a direct impact on the child's learning and understanding, so strategies for change are urgently needed.

Case Study 5

Getting parents involved and attending school functions was a continual issue in the school. The reasons were varied and not unlike those in other inner city schools. However, an opportunity arose to provide an innovative way to persuade parents into school, whilst at the same time addressing their anxiety about the 'mystique' of science. Because of my enthusiasm for science and its importance in helping children and adults understand the world around them I set up a community science club to be held once a week after school.

The club set out to encourage reticent parents into the school. Although the staff tried to bridge the gap between parental expectations and the reality of school life there was still a need to encourage more active participation by some of the parents. We had had some success with our evening and day sessions working with parents on curriculum areas, but science had always been the least popular of the three core curriculum areas – hence a science club for parents and their children. I identified some reasonably simple science activities which would be appropriate if there were some differentiated help for all ages, gathered the materials together, sent out an invitation to every family and waited. It was quite a gamble – if too many families turned up it would be difficult to run it successfully but if too few, we would feel frustrated.

Luckily, as seems to be the way of these things, about twenty children and their parents arrived. We had stipulated that children could only attend if accompanied by an adult. This seemed harsh but the central aim was after all to encourage parents into the school.

During the life of the club we attracted not only parents but also older siblings and grandparents. The older children who came in were there to collect their brothers or sisters on the way back from their own schools but, after some initial hesitation on both sides, the older children quickly became members of the club. Barriers were broken down – families who didn't generally get on with one another found themselves joining in the general management and delivery of the sessions. As well as a learning experience, it became a social event.

By the end of the first term the adults and older children were virtually running the club themselves. It was good to see so many adults revisiting science and finding themselves understanding the concepts and able to join in the learning with their children. The club became the social event of the week – a place where children and parents could work on imaginative science activities whilst at the same time forming new friendships among the mix of ages. Drinks, snacks and fruit were provided each week and during the summer months we worked on outdoor activities, including the school garden project. Also amazing was the way some of the mums forged ahead, acquiring scientific knowledge and revelling in the feelings of empowerment this brought.

The materials used in the science club were inexpensive and generally renewable but we did benefit from a generous input of materials and person power from the Royal Mail. A wonderful person who worked in their PR office arrived one day and offered to set up a darkroom facility in a spare small room. This allowed children and adults to do some photography and developing, and the early years children proved adept with a camera. A Millennium Fellowship awarded to me by the British Association for the Advancement of Science and the Millennium Commission enabled us to purchase additional equipment which was sustainable and also good for classroom use, including a weather station, additional computer equipment and cameras.

The Community science club was an immense success and has been replicated elsewhere in the form of Inspire Community Science Clubs. These clubs cater for the whole spectrum of the primary age range and are an effective means of working across the age groups with interested adults.

The activities evolve constantly. In the early days of the Inspire project a celebration day would be held in areas where the clubs were flourishing, so allowing ideas to be shared and future activities discussed. Workshops run by the participating schools helped to promote the idea of science in the community and the clubs are still in action in various parts of Britain.

Case Study 6

Although the Inspire Project had involved many early years children I still wanted to set up a project specifically for the early years. Accordingly I began working on a project with a nursery school in Newham. The school had a typical inner city intake – a diverse range of cultures and nationalities. The school was an exciting place. The staff were very committed, the children were happy and the headteacher had great vision. The school was well equipped, in material resources and staffing numbers, but had difficulty involving some of the parents in school life.

The role of parents in a child's learning is crucially important and it was felt that if nursery children were to derive all they could from their time there, their parents needed to be involved. We had to draw them in if we possibly could and the proposed project would be one strategy for doing so.

First Steps is a Science project intended for nursery age children working with their parents in an informal club like setting. It is designed to give young children their first experience of investigative science and at the same time raise the confidence of parents in their own ability to do Science.

In this trial project in Newham, the headteacher and staff identified the parents they felt would benefit or help other parents to benefit from the experiences on offer. The sessions were held once a week in the Parents' room. Taking the theme of the circus – a context children know – the project investigated toys and games. Each session took as its central theme one particular toy, either modern or historical.

We examined balancing bears and clowns, roundabouts, spinning tops, zoetropes, flicker books, jumping clowns, magnetic games, windmills, helicopters and kaleidoscopes. Each week the children were persuaded to make an appropriate toy and we looked up key words associated with each activity. Parents were given a follow up sheet suggesting ideas for extending the activity at home. I deliberately used easily obtainable resources and provided any equipment that was needed but difficult to get.

The project benefited greatly from the active involvement of at least one of the nursery staff each session, which meant that the work could also be carried back into the nursery teaching areas.

During the ten weeks of the project, the people taking part formed a self supporting unit. At least two of the mums who had initially found the whole process daunting and who weren't particularly comfortable mixing with the other parents, became hugely enthusiastic about working with their children in a meaningful way. The end of the pilot scheme coincided with an important anniversary in the life of the school and we filled a whole marquee with activities we had been doing over the past few weeks – a memorable event for all those who had been involved.

The primary object of the project was to stimulate and encourage scientific enquiry and to create a non-threatening atmosphere where parents could come and work with their children on a worthwhile piece of learning. Research continually points to the importance of the role of the adults in a child's life and to the child's own learning. Schools which have parental participation as a central part of their ethos generally produce happy, interested children who have the security of knowing that their school and home are working together.

Obviously the particular pattern we used works in areas where many of the adults don't have jobs, but it is possible for any school to run social events with a learning focus out of hours. The pilot scheme involved the childminders of two of the children who took part when the parents couldn't manage to attend, thus widening the circle of adults involved in the learning process. I used a wheeled chest to carry the equipment and this was stored in the Parents' room, ensuring that the resources I needed were all in one place and complete, so that sessions could run smoothly.

I repeated these ideas in various parts of the country, including a far-flung rural area of Aberdeenshire where, although cultural differences weren't as apparent, the children and adults I worked with faced problems such as poverty and remoteness. They too found the experience worthwhile – Fife has continued with the work and the original ideas are flourishing.

In order to build on the original work carried out in Newham and to make it self sustaining, I organised a number of training days in areas where several schools were interested. The training was attended by nursery teachers, nursery officers and in some cases interested parents. They tried out the various activities and worked with the large crate of equipment given to each school which participated. Everyone had the chance to share and build on their ideas and I was able to adjust the project accordingly.

I was particularly moved by the twilight session I organised in Aberdeenshire, where the schools taking part were scattered over many miles on a bleak peninsula centered on Peterhead. I arrived in a school on a dark, rainy night, feeling certain the attendance would be poor. But amazingly, all the teachers and interested parents taking part in the scheme quickly arrived and worked enthusiastically with the practical tasks, disappearing mysteriously afterwards, armed with their wheeled chest of resources. All the schools that sent a representative member of staff carried out a successful First Steps science project and some of them still do so.

These case studies indicate what can be done. However, there are many ways of encouraging and building up the confidence of anxious parents. Science appears to present unique problems for some parents and indeed teachers and yet this is easily overcome.

Although there are great demands upon the timetable in the early years classroom, with a little imagination and much enthusiasm it is still possible to devote special days during the term to activities based around a scientific theme. Pirates Day and Bread Day are just two of the days that worked well in our early years department. On both days we encouraged parental involvement and the wide range of cultural experiences that were revealed ensured that the events were remembered long afterwards as special.

Section 3
Knowledge and Understanding

6

Science and Literacy

This chapter explores the connections between Literacy and Science. Firstly, there is the special vocabulary of Science, which helps us understand specific scientific concepts. This vocabulary is introduced at appropriate times during children's development. Language plays an important part in learning science. It is difficult to imagine a scientific investigation that does not require some elements of literacy, be it the interaction of children with each other or with the teacher, or when recording results, or sharing the findings.

The specialist vocabulary used to describe certain scientific conventions is described as Scientific Literacy. Problems associated with using everyday vocabulary in a scientific context arise, for example the use of the words *light* or *force* will usually mean something different to a young child from the meaning accepted in a scientific context. The use of everyday words in a different setting can be more difficult for a young child to understand than words which are particular to a science, such as *magnets*. Young children like the sound of 'grown-up' words; Year 2 children investigating tadpoles in the school pond were thrilled to be told that the life cycle of such a creature is described as a metamorphosis. Although the word was too difficult for many of the group, some did use it appropriately and were able to transfer the concept when learning about the life cycle of butterflies. Children will usually acquire vocabulary when they are ready to deal with it – any earlier can confuse them.

We should certainly not patronise early years children by using 'baby' terms for scientific actions, but as good practitioners we should also be aware of whether a child is ready to understand certain terms or concepts. I admit I have been tempted to answer 'It's magic' when asked to explain a difficult scientific concept to a young child. But I have found as both teacher and

parent that it is usually better for things to be explained as fully as possible in a way that is accessible to the enquirer.

I still smile when I remember a journey with our two children many years ago. We were returning from our annual summer camping holiday in Dorset and the children were growing restless in the back of the car. Suddenly, son (aged 4) asked how babies were made. Daughter, three years older, immediately stopped reading. Their father launched, unhesitatingly and deadpan, into a careful, basic account of how babies are made. His training as a Head of science department in an all girls school meant he could explain such things in a forthright and unemotional manner and adjust it to fit the requirements of a 4 year old and 7 year old. The audience, who by then had collapsed into fits of giggles, quickly shifted their interest to something else. They had received an answer in words they could understand and this area of learning was gradually expanded in ways they could understand and were ready for. Feasey (2000) suggests a useful progression scale for children's scientific development:

3-4 year-olds

- Children describe what they see and what happens
- Children sequence what they talk about
- Children use everyday words
- Teacher introduces some scientific words

4-5 year-olds

- Children use everyday language
- Teacher continues to introduce scientific words which build on those introduced earlier
- Children are encouraged to use scientific words
- Scientific words are displayed around the classroom

5-6 year-olds

- Children retell experiences using a limited range of scientific words
- Children explore their own ideas and those of others orally
- Children begin to talk about cause and effect
- Teacher continues to introduce scientific words linked to class topics

6-7 year-olds

- Children describe events and ideas in detail
- Children begin to offer explanations for what they observe happening
- Children use appropriate scientific language in context.
- Children are able to relate cause and effect in science
- Children begin to use language of reflection

Early years settings are designed in such a way that scientific language can be developed in the existing space. Many settings have areas for imaginative play, such as the Home Corner, technology area, access to suitable ICT equip-

ment, sand and water trays, and outdoor areas which can be used for construction play, mini beasts investigation, group art work, storytelling and role playing. This list is not exhaustive and each setting has its own unique environment. But all can provide stimulating areas for the development of scientific learning, including the development of appropriate language.

During a recent final Block Practice I was thrilled to see the imaginative way an early years PGCE student had transformed the home corner in the reception class into a café. It was a familiar context for the children, as Holloway Road is full of interesting small cafes, run mainly by local South American or Chinese communities, and the children at the school are aware of them.

The trainee teacher created a café in the classroom because she wanted the children to learn about healthy eating. She arranged seating areas, menus etc and then discussed with the children the types of food they needed to be healthy. This entailed planning menus which the children would change daily on a rota basis. The food was made – out of play dough – the café opened and business began. With initial help and encouragement from the teacher and a little intervention the children ran the café themselves. The trainee teacher had created a situation where the children could work independently on an important topic: about the need for eating healthily and acquiring appropriate vocabulary within a meaningful context.

This is one example of how children can be given opportunities to learn scientific ideas and concepts. The school in question has an ethos of teaching and learning in imaginative and innovative ways and this starts in the early years so that young children behave in a scientific manner.

At the same school a former student of mine rang to ask me whether she could bring her Class 1 children into the University to meet me. The children had been talking about scientists and my erstwhile student decided it would be good for them to interview me. Never having described myself as a scientist but having stressed over the years that we are all scientists, I could hardly refuse. It was a thoroughly enjoyable session. The children had decided what questions to ask and I answered as best I could. Pictures were taken and the children recorded the event when they returned to school.

Teaching in this way needs careful planning and continual awareness and monitoring of individual children's understanding of the vocabulary offered. I am frequently reminded of times when I misunderstood certain words as a child. I was brought up in a family with strong non-conformist ideals, where mealtimes were preceded by a prayer of thanks. As a very young child I mumbled what I thought were the correct words: 'Thank you for the world so sweet, thank you for the food we eat, thank you for the birds that *sink*, thank you God for everythink.' I was bewildered at the need to be thankful for those poor birds who were in constant danger of drowning. The idea that my parents, who were great enthusiasts of nature, actually condoned such actions was just one of the mysteries of grown-ups. It never occurred to me to ask anyone about it so my unease continued for years.

Similarly, a friend of mine who was brought up in postwar Britain when talk about the War was common, had heard the word tank and how the tanks had entered a war zone, bulldozing everything in sight. After listening to a particularly lurid account given by one of her parents' friends she was terrified to go into the bathroom in case the tank over the lavatory started coming towards her.

Donaldson (1978) quotes Laurie Lee to illustrate the ambiguity that so often arises in child/adult conversations.

> I spent that first day picking holes in paper, then went home in a smouldering temper.
> 'What's the matter Love? Didn't he like it at school then?'
> 'They never gave me the presents.
> 'Present? What present ?
> 'They said they'd give me a present.'
> Well, now, I'm sure they didn't.'
> 'They did! They said: 'You're Laurie Lee, aren't you?
> Well just sit there for the present.'
> I sat there all day but I never got it.
> I ain't going back there again.'

Donaldson goes on to argue that although Laurie Lee was unable to understand what the teacher meant, the teacher also failed to realise that the child couldn't follow her instructions because of her ego-centric approach – not selfish but looking at the world from her standpoint and not recognising that a child would see things differently. Skilled practitioners are aware of the need to decentre, to see the world from the child's standpoint.

Anny Northcote (2006) asserts that

> Children learn a language because they need to communicate. They do this best from their peers in a context where language is used to find things out, get things done, question, show understanding and express thoughts and feelings. Modelling by peers and teachers has been shown to be the most effective way to engage children new to a language. Visual support and practical activities which are intellectually challenging provide a context for the language in which speakers and listeners can take an active role.

In this discourse, the importance of practical activity and modeling appropriate vocabulary for bilingual learners is seen as an essential component of the learning process. If children cannot use correct and appropriate vocabulary when describing an activity they have undertaken, it is easy to assume that they don't understand the concepts involved. Such mistaken assumptions are easily made about children who are working in a language that is not their first one. But bilingual children will most probably have understood what is going on. Nor should their lack of vocabulary to describe the work be equated with lack of ability. As Northcote (2006) argues, the process of learning two languages is in itself indicative of high ability. Bilingual learners learn more successfully if they are given a meaningful context within which to acquire knowledge and skills.

Assessing children's understanding of scientific activities often relies initially on their ability to communicate their findings so, inevitably, vocabulary is a vital aspect of the monitoring process. When children have yet to acquire all the relevant vocabulary, we need to look at other methods of assessing their learning and use other means of finding evidence. Children can be encouraged to draw about the activity or helped to write about it.

For children fully to benefit from scientific investigative work, practitioners need to use questioning appropriately. Teachers can effectively encourage children's investigation and understanding by asking the correct questions. Closed questions, requiring a Yes or No, are appropriate when introducing children to a new concept, as they foster confidence. But it is open ended questions that invite thoughtful responses and enable children ultimately to formulate their own predictions or hypotheses to investigate. *The Concept Cartoon Book* (Keogh and Naylor, 1996) offers excellent examples: the questions are about the cartoons, which show interesting scientific conundrums which will encourage children to raise questions. Cartoons naturally appeal to children and although some of the concepts are challenging, the younger children can work with an older or more able child or adult to answer the questions.

Literacy and science work mutually in developing learning when literacy is a part of a scientific investigation. Conversely, Science can be instrumental in delivering a certain aspect of Literacy. Many early years' story books, such as *The Very Hungry Caterpillar,* have scientific themes and these provide excellent opportunities for enriching the partnership of science and literacy.

This symbiotic link between Science and Literacy is strongest in Key Stage 1 and 2 where the timetable for science is limited by the time demanded for the Numeracy and Literacy hours. It is sad to see Science relegated to a small share of the timetable. PGCE students complain about being unable to 'do' science on their teaching practice because it wasn't on the schedule that half term. I had hoped this would be remedied by *Excellence and Enjoyment* (Primary National Strategy DfES). However Literacy and Numeracy still dominate timetable space, indicating that Science is still seen by our policy makers as of secondary importance. This is a great shame when children at Key Stage 1 and 2 are so receptive to learning about Science.

In the Foundation Stage the curriculum is approached holistically, the subjects interweaving one with another as they do in everyday life. This enables children in the Foundation stage to experience learning in a less contrived manner.

To enhance literacy/science work, we provide? we must take account of the differing needs of children at different ages. Early years children benefit from the scaffolding of their work through writing or talking frames – what its instigator, Bruner likened to scaffolding used in the building trade to assist the stability of a structure. Just as scaffolding is gradually dismantled as the building becomes sturdier, so the need to support a children's understanding is gradually withdrawn until they can work independently. A frame can help children to recount their work – either the teacher encourages the children to talk about their work or write or draw about it themselves using the information sheet provided in the scaffolding, which will vary according to the children's needs. For practical tasks, teachers model the method until the children feel confident to carry out the task themselves.

There are numerous other ways of encouraging young children to record their activities. The teacher can use children's drawings to generate discussion with the children about their content. Digital cameras, model making, role playing, short dramatic scenes can all be used to allow time for children to explain their understanding of a particular activity.

Another important means of recording is for children to sequence the activity correctly, using pictures or drawings of the activity. Early years children are encouraged to work on sequencing if they are given a sugar paper zigzag book – ideally about 6cms high as this allows for space for small hands to work in.

The next Case Study illustrates science and language working together.

Case Study 7

A group of Year 1 children had been working on patterns and colours. They had made their own spinning tops, using card circles and placing short pieces of dowling in the holes in the centre of the circles. They had been encouraged to colour the upper side of the card circles and then spin them as quickly as possible. By asking appropriate questions the teacher elicited a description of what was happening to the circle and the colours. She then replaced the card circles and dowling with Doodletops (small spinning tops that rotate on a felt tip pen, so leaving a trace of the patterns in which they spin) and asked the children to experiment with them on large pieces of sugar paper.

Sam: It's making a pattern like a snake.....

Amy: Mine is going round in a circle

Sam: My one is going slower. It's wobbling

Amy: My one is going slower now. Its making a bigger pattern

Sam: The big patterns come at the end

Amy: They come when it stops spinning

Sam: They fall on their side and start to roll

Amy: And then the pattern stops. It just gets a line

Sam: Shall we spin them again?

Amy: Let's spin them together. Mine will spin longer

Sam: No, mine will spin longer

Adult: Why do you think yours will spin longer?

Sam: My one went longer last time. It spins better

Amy: My one gives a better pattern. It's blue

Adult: Shall we see? I'll count down from three. Three. Two. One. Go

They watch.

Sam: Mine won. It's still spinning

Amy: That's not fair. Mine was on the paper which isn't smooth. It's already got lots of patterns on it

Adult: Do you want to try again?

They spin the doodle tops again, on a different section of paper.

Sam: Mine again!

Amy: Miss, miss, it's still not fair. He's spinning his more at the start

Adult: Shall I spin both of them for you? Will that be fairer?

The adult spins the two tops. This time Amy's top spins longest.

Sam: Miss, you wanted hers to win. You didn't spin mine as hard

Adult: Perhaps it was because your top was in my left hand. I'm not so good spinning with my left hand. Shall I swop them round

The children nod their assent. The adult spins the tops again.

This time Sam's spins longest.

Sam: The more spin you give it, the longer it spins.

Amy: And the faster you spin it, the more it stays in one place without making a pattern

Here we see science and literacy working together. Spinning a Doodletop provided a useful context for the children to use appropriate words to describe what they saw.

7
Science and Numeracy

Case Study 8

Reception class children in a North London primary school with a student teacher. The children had been working with their teacher on sinking and floating activities. They had already carried out an investigation to find out whether the items floated or sank using resources found in the classroom. The earlier work had involved predicting or guessing about the properties of each item and then testing out their predictions. Grouping for science sessions was deliberately mixed, with varied abilities in each group. The carefully planned deployment of other adults in the room enabled the student teacher to work with small groups on the raft investigation.

The group were given a paper raft the teacher had made earlier. After discussing about floating and sinking in light of the work they had already done the children were asked to guess or predict how many marbles they could put into the craft before it sank.

Student: How many marbles do you think we'll be able to put in the boat before it sinks?

Tommy: Ten

Salina: Two

Carlton: Four

Student: Shall we try? Shall we take turns putting the marbles in?

They each put a marble in the boat, then another is added making six in all.

Has it sunk yet?

Salina: No

Carlton: Let's put lots of marbles in our raft

Student: Why don't you each count five more and put them in. Carlton, you go first.

Carlton: One. Two. Three. Four. Five.

Student: Still floating. Now you, Salina.

Salina: One. One. One. One. One.

Student: Still floating. Your go, Tommy.

Tommy: One. Two

Tommy is becoming bored waiting for his turn and starts throwing the marbles at the raft.

Salina: Miss, miss, he shouldn't throw them.

Student: Why not? Why shouldn't he throw them?

Salina: He'll break our boat

Student: Do you think Salina is right?

Carlton: Yes, miss.

Student: So they are all the same. Do you see why Tommy?

Tommy does not respond.

Student: Come on Tommy. You've got to finish your go. Where did we get to?

Carlton: He's done two. It's three next.

Student: Tommy, will you put your last three in?

Salina: Miss he's putting them all in.

Student: Well, he's done it now. And the boat is still floating.

Carlton: It's still well afloat. You could get loads more in.

Student: Shall we try ten this time? Tommy, do you want to go first?

Tommy is still reluctant, but picks up a handful of marbles.

He puts them in one at a time, counting to himself.

Carlton: That was only nine.

Student: (Does a quick count). No, I think there were ten. You have a go now, Carlton.

Carlton adds ten marbles, counting them carefully.

Student: Salina, your go. Shall we count together?

Salina adds ten marbles.

The three children chant the numbers from one to ten as she does so.

Carlton: It's going into the water

Tommy: Its much lower in that corner where all the marbles are.

Salina: I think it will sink soon.

Student: Shall we put some more marbles in? Five more each?

Tommy: Ten more.

Student: All right, count ten each. Salina, you go first this time.

Salina adds her marbles, and the children count.

Carlton: It's nearly sunk now.

Student: Will it hold any more? We'll have to be very careful. Tommy, you'll have to put them in very carefully.

Tommy: One. (Long Pause). Two (Long Pause) Three.....

Student: Its nearly sunk now. Look, the water is just coming over the side......

Tommy: Four-five-six-seven-eight-nine-ten. Sunk it!

The activity continued until the raft finally sank. The children decided to count up all the marbles that had sunk it. The results were recorded onto a simple database programme on the classroom computer.

The children talked about the numbers, comparing the figures to the guesses they had made before starting the experiment. The findings led to further discussion.

This activity illustrates how numeracy skills can be used to enhance a science activity. Although the concept of floating and sinking is fairly complex, the teacher was able to devise an investigation the children could relate to. It was a game and involved lots of water and mess, the context was familiar and felt comfortable, and they were all actively engaged.

> Mathematical development depends on becoming confident and competent in learning and using key skills. (CGFS, p68)

Mathematical skills and scientific skills are similar: predicting, experimenting, recording, communicating. For children to be able to carry out a scientific investigation they require a basic understanding of number. The two areas of the curriculum are closely linked. Many science activities involve developing skills at sorting, measuring, counting, ordering. At times Numeracy suffers the same bad press as science does. Adults who had unsatisfactory experiences of maths in their school days may pass on their negative attitudes towards the subject to their children. So Mathematics and Science together can appear daunting, but by using the one subject to enhance the other, the outcome can be good. And the process skills required are similar for both subjects. Because so many of the investigative skills we associate with science are found in successful Numeracy investigations and vice versa, providing useful and interesting scientific investigations encourages young children to use their numeracy skills.

Case study 9
The children in this inner city primary school in the North West of England, are from the nursery and reception classes. They are members of the Community Science club (see Chapter 5) which has been running for two terms. Initially operated by the science co-ordinator, it is now run by interested parents, although the science co-ordinator remains available. The club is attended by children from most years in the school, plus a few older siblings from the local comprehensive.

The investigation is to find out the best way to balance a card bear, using metal washers. This is part of a series of investigations around Forces. Jo is a Nursery child and the helper Rashida is a Year 6 child.

Jo: I'm going to put lots of rings on my clown

Rashid: Why are you putting so many on?

Jo: So he'll stay on the string.

Rashid: (*puts clown on string*). Whooo... (clown falls to floor) Why did that happen?

Jo: He slipped

Rashid: Shall we try again? (*puts clown on string again. It falls off again*). Why doesn't he balance?

Jo: He's got too many on one side. He falls down on the side where the rings are.

Rashid: Shall we move the rings?

Jo: Yes

Rashid: All of them?

Jo: (*Pause*). Lets move that one. And that one

They move two washers

Rashid: Does it balance now?

Jo: (*clown leans to one side*) He's still falling over

Rashid: Shall we move any more rings?

Jo: Yes.   That one. Then he'll have four on each side.

They move the washer and put the clown on the string. It balances.

Jo: Yes. Yes. Ms James come and look at my clown. Look, look, he stays on the string with all those rings...

In this observation we again see the younger child making use of scientific and numerical skills. The concept of balance is fairly complex but Jo can experiment with the idea, using card bears which are recognisable and meaningful to most children, and also using counting with a purpose – the purpose of finding the ideal number to help balance the bear.

Bears and other familiar toys are appropriate tools for delivering quite complex scientific concepts. Broadbent, Patilla and Montague-Smith's (1994) *Compare Bears: Science and Technology* describes how a set of toy bears can be used to deliver scientific and technological ideas in interesting ways. The need to embed new experiences within a meaningful context for children is central to teaching effectively in the early years. This is reinforced by Feasey and Gallear (2000):

> A key issue in science is that the teacher should raise the profile of the application of number in this curriculum area. The use of mathematics in science offers its own beauty as well as challenges. It also provides powerful evidence upon which new knowledge can be developed by both children and adults.

Children begin learning about measurement by using qualitative terms such as biggest and smallest, tallest and shortest. Then they move on to comparatives such as bigger and smaller or faster and slower. The next step is non standard measurements – for example using their hands and feet, or marbles, or Compare Bears to measure things in an investigation. Finally, children are ready for and see the reason for standard measurements.

8
Science and Technology

Case Study 10

On a warm sunny day two Year 1 children are making boats. They are excited at the prospect of creating a 'real' boat that will sail right across the paddling pool. They have already tried to sail their boats across the pool by just placing them in the water and waiting, but as this soon becomes frustrating, the teacher suggests they look at some of the toy boats in the classroom. The children examine these boats and notice that one of them has a paddle at one end. The teacher talks with the children about its function and they decide to try out the paddle boat in the paddling pool. The boat moves quite briskly across the water and the children then decide to try to construct something similar.

Jeffrey and Sarfraz have made boats out of plastic bottles held together with elastic bands. Around the neck of the bottle boats they have put another elastic band into which they can insert a paddle.

Jeffrey: This one is going to get to the other side of the pool.

Sarfraz: It won't. You need a bigger paddle. Like this one.

They wind up their paddles, then let the boats go.

Both boats stop in the centre of the pool.

Sarfraz: Told you. You need a big paddle.

Jeffrey: Yours didn't get there.

Sarfraz: I didn't wind mine as much as yours.

Jeffrey: You did. You were winding for longer.

Sarfraz:	(*Raising voice*) Didn't, didn't.
Adult:	Why don't you count how many times you wind it?
Jeffrey:	I did mine a hundred times
Sarfraz:	Miss, he didn't.
Adult:	Well, why don't you both wind yours forty times and see how far they go?

They wind the paddles while counting.

Adult:	Did you count each time you turned the paddle?
Both:	Yes.

Adult: Okay, put them both in the pool. Hold them at this side of the pool. Go.

Jeffrey: Mine went further.

Sarfraz: He gave his a big push. That's not fair.

Adult: Yes, it's not fair to help your boat.

Jeffrey: Mine went further anyway.

Sarfraz: He's got a bigger paddle.

Adult: You can have a bigger paddle if you want. There are lots in the box.

Sarfraz: I want the red one.

Adult: But the blue one is bigger...

Sarfraz: I want this one.

Adult: Okay. Let's wind them up carefully and test them again. Do fifty turns this time.

They try both boats again. This time Sarfraz's boat does reach the other side.

Jeffrey: He's cheated. He must have wound it up more.

Sarfraz: No I never.

Adult: But we counted when you wound them up. What else might make a difference?

Jeffrey: His boat is a different shape. Mine has got all squashed.

Adult: Why don't you try some more bottles? That might make a difference. And are you both using the same type of elastic band? That might make a difference.

Sarfraz: Can we take these home?

Adult: I don't think your mum will thank me for sending home two wet bottles. Have you got any bottles like this at home?

Sarfraz: Loads.

Adult: You could easily make one of these at home. Your mum or your dad might help.

Jeffrey: My grandad's looking after me tonight. He'll help me.

This activity took place in a class where the children had been working on floating and sinking. They made their boats in the final session, thus combining science and technology. To make a boat that would move required

technology. Although the children had carried out various investigations into floating and sinking before, they had never produced their own vessels. By bringing in the idea of making the boat move, the teacher introduced the children to an aspect of technology they hadn't encountered before.

The children continued to refine their models and were soon joined by other children in the class who wanted to make their own boats. Jeffrey and Sarfraz were able to act as peer tutors to the other children and this unplanned part of the session worked well. The two children extended their own understanding when showing other children how to produce a successful boat (peer and paired tutoring is discussed in chapter 4).

The activity was a great success and the children went on to look at other methods of making their boats move. Children learn best when the learning takes place within contexts with which they are familiar, and the paddling pool added to the excitement.

Case Study 11

The setting is a nursery class in South London. The teacher is keen to introduce early years children to useful tools and equipment as soon as possible. A group of children now entering their second year in the nursery are shown how to use various tools: scissors, rulers, junior hacksaws, bench hooks, glue guns. The tools are introduced carefully and the safety rules for each are discussed.

For the children to feel confident about using such equipment it is useful for them to encounter the items as appropriate. Some early years teachers are still reluctant about letting young children use such equipment. My personal experience has confirmed that it is safe and productive to allow controlled access to tools early on.

The teacher encourages the children to use the tools and experiment with them, on the understanding that certain basic rules must be observed or the tool will be taken away. Obviously the success of these activities will depend at this age on the fine motor skills of each child. If, for example, a child can't use a pair of scissors correctly they will probably have difficulty in using a saw and bench hook. As with all teaching, the teacher provides opportunities for the children which she thinks they are capable of achieving, possibly with some help.

To place the activity in context, the teacher suggests that the children think about the birds that visit the garden. Although the school is the inner city, birds frequently visit its gardens. The teacher begins discussions with the children about why the birds visit and a child answers eagerly that the birds come for food. This boy lives on the third floor of a tower block but he and his mum frequently put crumbs out for the birds. He knows that the big fat pigeons try to eat all the food but that some of the smaller birds move very quickly and sometimes manage to get there first.

The teacher then goes on to discuss how they could encourage more birds into their nursery garden. Another child suggests that they could throw crumbs on the ground but someone else says that they have seen cats chasing after the birds. With gentle intervention and encouragement from their teacher, the children decide to build a bird feeding table. They are shown pictures of tables and decide to draw one for themselves. After more discussion the children decide on which table to make. One child is unhappy that her idea wasn't chosen but is persuaded to join in the construction.

The teacher helps the children to cut pieces of plastic corrugated sheeting (Correx) to make a table top. They know how to use the glue gun safely and understand why they must wear safety goggles. One member of the group helps the teacher to stick the pieces together. The schoolkeeper, a keen ornithologist who likes to encourage the children to take an interest in birds, provides a suitable post for the bird table to sit on. The bird table is installed in the garden and the children crowd around it expectantly, waiting for the first birds to come and try the food. But they are disappointed. After a few minutes of frustration, three of the group wander off to another activity but two remain and start talking about ways of attracting the birds to their table. Again, careful open ended questioning by the teacher elicits the response that they need to hide if they want to see the birds.

The activity continued with the children building a hide in the garden where they could watch the birds. They made it from old blankets thrown over two adult chairs. A hole was cut in one blanket, so the children could observe the table and, ultimately, its visitors.

In this example of D&T and science working together, the children learned about the feeding habits of birds, identified a need for a safe feeding area and then continued to refine their ideas to make the successful bird table.

The relationship between Science and Technology

Science and technology are inextricably linked. The introduction of a formal curriculum in English schools in the late 1980s treated them as two discrete subjects but in practice they exist almost as one. The CGFS document acknowledges their inter-relationship and many links are made between them in the KUW section. Siraj-Blatchford and Macleod-Brudenell (1999) argue that such a cross curricular approach is how early years children experience their learning as this is how they learn in the home setting, across the whole spectrum of subjects rather than in clearly defined 'subjects'.

Howe (2003) argues that in addition to the KUW area, science and D&T occur throughout all the areas of learning in the Foundation Stage.

> It is often said that 'science and D&T are in Knowledge and Understanding of the World'... However, in my view there is not quite such a straightforward correlation between 'subjects' and 'areas of learning'.

With the introduction of the Excellence and Enjoyment strategy of 2003 the question of cross curricular links has been revisited – the Primary strategy has enabled schools to provide a more coherent approach to curriculum planning and, one hopes, to provide a richer education for all young children. Yet at the time of writing it is apparent that many schools are unwilling to embrace cross curricular teaching on grounds that this will not allow sufficient time for Literacy and Numeracy. They are still adhering to a formal subject based approach so as to prepare their pupils for the summative assessments of SATs.

English (2001) sums up how children best learn and understand:

> Children need to develop understanding in order to make connections with what they already know, to solve problems, to be creative, to reason, to make sense of what they are learning and, because of this, remember what they have learned and apply that learning in new contexts.

There is a mantra among science educators: 'I hear and I forget, I see and I remember, I do and I understand'. It is supposedly a Chinese proverb, although cynics suggest it was devised by a group of science educators at a conference in the 1960s. But it does encapsulate the learning process both in school and out.

Most children are regularly employing design technology and scientific skills long before the terms are used to describe their activities. Children come to the early years setting with many skills already developed. Most will have had chance to play with toys and objects in the home. Many children want to discover how things work and will have started taking things apart, sometimes to the dismay of parents, who didn't really want the bedroom clock in pieces. We saw it with our own children – both preferred playing with pots and pans out of the cupboard than with the expensive building blocks bought by generous grandparents. They would devise amazing tents in the garden and spend hours in them with their friends. Our daughter would work out what was needed for domestic comfort, such as clothes' dryer, curtains, cups, torch etc and then she and her younger brother would create their home.

I can still remember my brothers' and my favourite pastime, long before I started school. We would set up a grocery shop in the kitchen. Mum willingly lent us anything in her pantry that would help us to create a shop. Building stacked up shelves by balancing wooden planks on tins, writing out price tags, using an old toy till in which to collect the money, were all part of the game. Plenty of skills came into it: building with a purpose, refining our shop design, designing price tags, counting money and, perhaps most importantly, learning how to negotiate with two siblings over which roles to play. Although I didn't realise at the time that I was witnessing a technological miracle, I was the unwilling observer of the demise of my doll's pram and its transformation into the go kart that my brothers had decided to build out of it. But one could say it was certainly an excellent example of identifying a need and then sourcing the materials and building the desired object.

When they first come to school it is important to build on the skills children have already acquired at home. Many of the skills and processes used in science work are also needed in design and technology. Children need to be encouraged to design, create and evaluate a project, albeit informally at the Foundation stage.

CGFS (2000) p 91 in KUW states that practitioners should

- Provide opportunities for children to practice their skills, initiate and plan simple projects and select, choose and devise their own solutions in design and making processes

- Extend range of techniques such as cutting (scissors, pastry cutter, moulds, tearing), joining (adhesives, stapling, masking tape, treasury tag, paper clip, paper fastener, elastic band, sewing) and finishing (crimping, weaving, tufting, pleating, painting and colouring)

- Encourage use of evaluative and comparative language, for example 'longer', shorter', 'lighter', 'heavier' and 'stronger'.

When children enter Class 1 these skills are developed further. NC (Design and Technology at Key Stage 1) has four main components:

- Developing, planning and communicating ideas

- Working with tools, equipment, materials and components to make quality products

- Evaluating processes and products

- Knowledge and understanding of materials and components

Full days of science and D&T can be built around such themes as the Circus, or Pirates. Such topics provide many opportunities for combining these two areas of the curriculum.

9
Resources

'Where do you get all these wonderful resources?' I'm frequently asked when I'm at science festivals or have taken an activity into a school. 'Don't you need lots of specialist equipment to teach science?' What I hope this book shows is that wonderful resources for science are all around you, and no, you don't need masses of specialist equipment to teach it.

In fact, if you have to reach for the specialist catalogues and start ordering from the pages headed 'Science', you're quite likely to be heading off in the wrong direction. Science teaching and learning is at its best when you use everyday, familiar items the children can immediately place in context. Get the science out of whatever comes easily to hand, and don't try and force teaching into strange avenues with the forbidding label 'Science'.

If you have to buy a set of materials for a specific science activity, chances are they'll be relatively expensive. Then you'll be faced with a couple of un-palatable alternatives – either get one (or a few) and briefly show them to the children, or get enough for everybody, but tell everyone to be careful, because you have to collect them back at the end. If you do the former, the children don't get a chance to interact with the materials. If you resort to the latter, the children don't interact with them properly, for fear of dropping, breaking or using up whatever it is.

What you need are plenty of robust, cheap, colourful building blocks and toys. Probably exactly the sort of thing you already have in your classroom. Supplement this with card, plastic sheets, wood, paper and elastic bands, so children can engineer artefacts that can be taken home. That way, you will not only enhance children's understanding of science but will be well on the way to educating their parents, too about science.

The final comment about where to get your resources is this: I keep an eye out all the time. One of the best resources I've used with pre-school children is a set of *Thomas the Tank Engine* books. When you slide a volume from its jacket, it unfolds to reveal a small model world, with a railway track and a tiny engine just waiting to be wound up and set on its way. How many times will Thomas go round the track if we wind him up five times? How many laps if we wind him ten times?

I'd seen these in bookshops but considered them over-priced at £17.50. Then, in Edinburgh one August for the festival, we wandered into a discount book store to escape a sudden shower. There was a stack of these books, at a bargain £3 each. They had 17 copies in stock, and I bought the lot.

Six years on and these unwanted little books are still doing valuable service, introducing topics on clockwork or balance to young children, serving as props for older children first taking on peer work, and fascinating whole gatherings of teachers on inset courses.

Rooms

Do primary schools need laboratories? Of course they do – but what is a laboratory? The word comes from the Latin *laboratorium*, meaning 'a place to work'. So a small primary school will probably have at least eight 'places to work'. They're called classrooms.

Ideally they should have running water, and access to that even larger laboratory known as the outside world. But even access to a hall is good. Halls make superb science and technology laboratories, because there is so much space and, unlike the great outdoors, rain rarely interrupts activities. Just remember to sweep up afterwards, before the deputy's class uses the place for PE.

Construction kits

Construction kits are a cornerstone of the early years classroom. There are different types of kits, and all have their merits and de-merits. However, it is probably worth settling on just one or two, because the one thing kits don't have is inter-compatibility, and once the systems start getting mixed up you'll have some very frustrated pupils.

Lego is the big name. Its great advantage is its virtual universality, so most children are familiar with it and will know how to put it together. But that is also a disadvantage, because children with Lego at home may well be tempted to extend their own sets with a pocketful from school. Wouldn't happen with your children, but watch those Y6 pupils who come over to help...

The other disadvantage of Lego, and its scaled up relative Duplo, is that it is expensive. There are some cheaper generic bricks, such as Megablox, which do fit with Lego, but they are rarely available from educational suppliers so have to be purchased from a commercial store and reimbursement sought – which is not always easy. Megablox are made from softer plastic than Lego, so pieces can be drilled if, for example, you want a brick that would hold a piece of wooden dowel. I have made masts for toy boats like this – you can then slide a piece of Correx onto the dowel to make a sail.

Children should be encouraged to use Lego as a prototyping tool. That is, you go and build something in Lego, then use your Lego model to guide you while you build a second model from cheaper components. If you allow their Lego

– or any other construction kit – model to be the end product, putting their model on display reduces the amount of kit available for other investigations. This can be a problem even for well equipped schools, when twenty or thirty Lego houses go on display.

Sand and water

Sand and water trays are the great glory of the early years classroom. A pity they aren't a standard feature of all primary classrooms. Instant test arenas for vehicles and boats, they also help develop essential understanding of solids and liquids, ideas about flow, and about actions and consequences – for example, dropping sand through a sand-wheel to produce movement.

Many nursery classes have a paddling pool. This is generally brought out on one or two really hot days each year for the children to play in but languishes at the back of the stock-room for the rest of the year. Why not use it as an extended water tray, a test area for large boats? You won't need the same depth of water as you do for paddling, just enough to get the boats off the bottom – a few centimeters will do. So it will require less filling and emptying.

Where you set it up requires careful thought. The schoolkeeper won't thank you for having it indoors. In an open playground it will be a nuisance unless you have a rota of adults to supervise it throughout the day. Assembly may be quick, but filling it might take time, even with a hose. And think about where the water will go when you empty it.

Rigid frame pools make much better 'testing tanks' than blow-up pools. When children lean on the sides of a blow-up pool – which they will – to retrieve their boats, the wall gives way and water spills out. The best rigid frames I have found are Quadro pools, and these have the advantage that they can be connected into other Quadro systems.

Plastic bottles

If you are using a paddling pool, plastic bottles are really good for building boats (see pages 22-25). Two 2-litre soft drinks bottles, held side by side with elastic bands, will form a buoyant and stable platform. Children can then assemble all sorts of sails and superstructure on top of this base. Older Key Stage 1 pupils will also be able to cope with building a motor and air-screw propeller arrangement to blow the boat along. But don't try to build a propeller that works in the water – the mechanical arrangements are too complex.

Magnets

Children undoubtedly need to experience traditional horse-shoe magnets. But magnets need to be looked after. If they aren't kept in boxes with the little metal 'keepers' fitted in place, the magnetism leaks away.

Less well known, but more impressive, are ceramic magnets. These tend to be smaller, more robust and more powerful. My box of them has been knocked, shaken and generally neglected for over six years and they still attract and repel in a satisfying magnet-like manner. Ceramic magnets tend not to be used in primary schools because they appear to contradict the principle that iron is magnetic and magnets are only made of iron. Ceramic magnets work by having small pieces of magnetic iron mixed into the ceramic before firing – and they last well because the magnetic material is held inside the ceramic, so doesn't lose magnetism every time the material is knocked.

You can get ceramic magnets from Ivydale Science Centre and elsewhere.

Marbles and beads

Marbles make excellent weights. They are relatively heavy and have identical weights, so you can count the numbers needed to sink a boat, and then compare with the number needed for another boat.

They have two disadvantages:

- Young children may put marbles in their mouths, so don't use them unsupervised. Also check local authority advice, as one or two have draconian bans in place.

- Marbles drop on the floor and roll under things. There is no great problem with losing them – they are cheap enough. The danger is that children moving after them in an effort to catch them might collide with furniture. And marbles which escape are a hazard – people might slip on one.

Wooden beads are less likely to be ingested and you can find shaped beads that don't roll away easily. They are excellent for sorting and counting, but they are not as heavy as marbles, so are less useful for investigating forces and similar effects.

Cans

Cans are useful as props in making shops, and also great for rolling down slopes. Thanks to new can technology in the last ten years, slightly tapered cans are now used by most food manufacturers. Because they are slightly narrower at the base, they fit neatly onto the slightly wider top of the can below. This means they stack more securely on supermarket shelves, but it also means that they don't roll in straight lines but with an inward curve towards the base. This will surprise adults brought up on the received wisdom that cans roll in straight lines.

You can still find older style cans, usually in smaller stores. You can recognise them by their raised edges at both ends of the can. It may be worth laying in a small stock of both types, to let children investigate the difference between them. It is also quite fun to investigate the behaviour of cans with different contents – cans with fairly solid contents, like dog food, roll much further than cans with liquid contents, like soup. But only use a very gentle slope, or the cans roll too far to measure.